MW01058913

MID DRIFT

Mid Drift

Copyright © 2011 by Kate Hanson Foster

ISBN 978-0-931507-27-4

Printed in the United States of America
First Edition

Designer: Dennis Ludvino
Printer: Thomson-Shore, Inc.

Loom Press
P.O. Box 1394
Lowell, Massachusetts 01853
www.loompress.com
info@loompress.com

The cover image is a detail from Peter Gourfain's sculpture *Stele
for the Merrimack (1996),* located in Tremont Yard near the Western
Canal along Suffolk Street in Lowell, Massachusetts. The sculpture
commemorates the wide variety of life generated by the Merrimack
River. The four sides of this work include images of flora and fauna
supported by the river, along with those of the people who have
depended on the river throughout history.

MID DRIFT

Poems by Kate Hanson Foster

CONTENTS

PRAYER

Along the Riverwalk,

refuse skirts the southern bank.

White foam pools below

the cantilever. I've come here

because I don't expect to be found.

Dear God:

what should we make

of what has gone wrong with my life?

All day I could watch

dead water. I'm in love

with a lunatic, I drink too much,

and I no longer believe in recovery.

I want back what disappears

into the crook of the canal.

Dear God:

this is my persistent letter,

my pinched bead,

my hymn that tolls and darkens,

this is my church bell shaking

off the birds.

MILL CITY

No human echo—
Just a hum that drips from the street

wires, a pulse that lets loose
from the glass of vacant storefronts.

My mind is filthy with old, dear secrets.
Another room sinks into its pine boards

and someone comes to assign value;
pull sewage out of the canal.

So much left over from so much
ordinary life.

I am seduced
by the red x on buildings

where no one bothers. Another ceiling
gives in, and my gutters fill.

It is the unlit room,
the windowpane that keeps hold

of that flat ochre light.
It is absence.

And not even post and beam can escape
the flutter of that grey wing.

A crack opens another foundation —
Something in the flesh trying to beat its way out.

Just watch it go.

RIVERWALK

The mile-long path along the Merrimack
ends at the Aiken Street Bridge.

He tells me about his drinking
problem, the prostitute,

his unhappy marriage.
A stickler for facts, he informs me

this is the longest lenticular
truss bridge remaining in the United States.

I tell him I can sometimes still see Tom
hanging from the cast iron.

JUNE, ON THE AIKEN
STREET BRIDGE

In some hour of June I imagine
the hugeness of the night. Wild lines

of trees, ash ridden doorways,
and somewhere behind

the cool thickness of brick
you simply jumped —

veins swelling a river of black
poisons, your final hours written in water.

In the city things continued
to breathe, yellow marigolds dripped with dew,

and I imagine clusters of foam collected
like a blanket just below you.

We rarely speak of you now.

SOMETIMES

I still picture him with that prostitute.
driving through the gate past the parking attendant,

neon lights shining the color of sour
milk into the back seat. His bare

ass or her low-sagging breasts. And then
the awkward fumbling, the condom wrapper,

the amount of time he takes to finish.
Sometimes the moans are real,

sometimes they are not. I wonder
what he says to her as he drops her off

at the boardinghouse, or later to himself
at a bar where he washes down her scent.

In other versions,
there is no parking garage. Instead,

we are parked in a lot by the edge of the river
passing a bottle back and forth.

Something that bites
on the way down. Sometimes I pretend

he never even told me the story,
and I am slowly slipping on my shoes again,

fastening the last button on my sweater.
And when he drops me off, sometimes

the excuse is never I don't know
why I did it but I did.

MAJOR'S

I remember this bar
only it was called something different —
I was underage, we hadn't met yet,
it doesn't matter.

You tell me
how you once placed my photograph
in a copy of James Wright's *Above The River*
and then returned it to the library.
Because you loved me.
Because I had recommended it
to you.

I want to tell you
about the time I sat next to your wife
at a bar. How awkward it was, silently drinking
side by side, like two empty households.

But I do not say anything.
I did not mean to come
to this bar again.

At this hour
the light makes a shadow out of everyone.

I remember that.

THE CLOCK TOWER

We were not supposed to be there,
but still he led me
up the spiral stairwell,
hands brushing
over the dust of the cast iron,
air thickening as we climbed the clock
tower built so high
it can be seen
from almost every mill yard.
When we reached the top
he took my picture.
To this day I cannot
say what I was after.

THE MERRIMACK

The moon is nothing

more than a clump of broken yellow,

the same moon that lights the silver

on the arching low branch, the fire

in my belly. You are home to me,

and I follow you with sloppy knees. Bare feet

pay no heed to the slimy bank, the bicycle

corroding, and to my surprise, your sleeves

make no ripples in the water.

CONFESSION

It's the same thing
every morning, that old man
sitting on the corner of Stevens
and Pine. His quart of milk
hidden in a brown paper bag.
I feel like he looks right at me, I say.
But I'm probably the only one who
looks — the way these cars pass
so indifferent, he may as well
be a statue of Jesus — arms outstretched
as if hugging the traffic in unison.
I think he's homeless, I say,
my voice heavy with concern,
I don't think I've ever seen pants
so dirty. And then we discuss
how sad it is. Unfortunate.
What time will the milk change
to whiskey. I say *I feel*
sorry, as if I've never felt anything
up until this very moment.
Not saying what I mean to say —
I think it's sexy the way he sits
like he has the whole damn city
to himself.

WOODWORKER

What you need
you can make with your own bare

hands. I move like a draft
around the house. You adore

me despite how I hate
my belongings, our two bodies

among objects — every shape
a solid pang that burns me

to the pith. You promise me
we do not bore each other

and run your plane along
the cutting edge, stripping

down to the smoothest point.
This is how things are done.

FROM THE BEDROOM

he calls, coils
of his voice

from the bedsprings,
my name repeating—

I don't answer.
I am only a body

treading across the carpet
beginning things

I will never finish,
a couple dishes left in the sink,

a pile of dust
on the kitchen floor,

and then I let the teabag grow cold—
just a few puffs of steam

and then none.
He emerges from the room

touching the bare, half-moon
of skin around my waist, the milky patch

he says is soft, like the skin of a lip,
the fold of an eyelid.

Where are you? he asks,
salt of sleep still thick

in his mouth. And I answer
the way a name is called

in a classroom, awkward
and distantly, *Here*.

LOVE

What the mouth does
is ordinary.

It is easy to live this way —

to let drop

what falls from our hands,
to kick what we are too tired to carry.

There is no masterpiece.

DRIVING HOME

I can't wait
for this season

to tear down
the leaves.

Nothing
should have an address.

PRAYER

With my knees on the floor
I feel for something missing.

This is not that story —
the one with a girl kneeling beside a bed

pleading to Saint Anthony, *Please
look around.* A lost necklace.

A holy language — the magic trick.
Wherever I turn, something unfastens

itself from my body.
Do not mistake me,

this is not that story of a Saint's flesh
gone completely corrupt

leaving only the bright red meat
of a tongue —

I can hardly speak
to such an absence. The words

are awkward — misshapen
in my mouth. Dear God:

the need is to leave
the loss where I have found it.

EVE'S FAITH

The truth of it: nothing
spoke to me. The body

was never mine — a ripple
under the skin,

a small bone dressed in wind.
I confess, my chest

was empty — clean
like the open eye of a wasp.

Let the prints
of my fingers unravel.

Lay me down in a pit
of broken fruit skins.

I do not want proof
of my life.

THE LOST TOMB OF JESUS

I want to touch
everything the light touches,

finger moving over mineral crust,
limestone, the signature

of a body patched in dust.
I want my breath to begin where his ended.

What if there are no bones
in heaven? What if

sifting through the sand reveals a shard
of an eye socket, a flake of rib

or a fossilized cheekbone sunken
into this rock shelf? I need something

that says the tomb sealed
shut, and even the birds forgot the light

that pinched out of every crevice,
that no eyes could see the shroud

creasing as the body slowly gave in,
because here I am

unearthing the hillside
and I don't even feel watched.

MY MOTHER'S FAITH

I was not prepared for God
to fill the house, flaming,

petal-winged, clash of air
and light. But how did I live

otherwise? I move from room
to room, each limb speaking

a new language no longer needing
proof of their liquid weight.

How lucky this is,
this sense of fullness —

I think I could place my hand inside
the stove and feel nothing.

I close my eyes, and Jesus pierces
my lids clean, his face

coiled in me
like a fingerprint.

OUR FATHER

never went to church
except on special occasions:
my First Communion,
Hannah's Confirmation.

He'd sit with hands unfolded,
knees poking out of the pew.
Everyone knew he wasn't Catholic.
No holy words took shape in his mouth.

Our father's father
shot himself in the head,
parked in his pickup outside a golf course.
He didn't play golf, my mother said,
it was so that someone would find him.

Afterwards, I stopped seeing his face
without the hole. I imagined
that somewhere in his lips a *Hail Mary* stuck
to the ash of the bullet, pushed back in
by the force of the gunshot.

Our father once said
he didn't believe in God
and that death was just a bag with no light
inside, a black bug in your coffin,
the stopping of all effort.

One time, during a fight with my mother,
he even said, *maybe*
I'd be better off dead — a panic
we later pressed against our chests
until the church went quiet,
the prayer finished.

MY FATHER AND HIS GUITAR

The desire
is to let these bones spill

into ruin. When she comes back
to my fingers, I press

loosely against her slight
tremble, her thin

wisps whisper and pull like a chest
that keeps rising.

SIBYL GROWING SMALLER

There is face I cannot make out
in the basin. A hangnail

that slowly unravels
finger, wrist, arm,

torso, one side of the body
dissolving into the other.

Do you want to know my future?
My final inch

will be this palm until even the veins
are flecked with gray, a body

closing in on itself, smell of skin
and gravel, and then the hair

blows off— tiny grains
of cells scattering,

only a voice aloft in liquid
air like panic, like warning.

GRANDMOTHER

The news is your memory is nothing
more than a dead weight. You hunch in your chair,
mind not quite dead, but always a little less than the last visit.

Mom says you don't talk much. It is your hands
that speak now, nervously moving
with the cursive fluttering of a moth.

I never thought I'd want your body to die,
the slow machine of you, sack of air
and murmur with pills melting into a stomach.

But I am impressed by its refusing,
each morning, when they unstick you
from the bed and move you to a window.

There must be evidence of you somewhere.
Before the strange forgetting,
the diagnosis, before the nurses,

there was woman standing in the kitchen,
smoke coiling from a cigarette.
There was the soft hum of a voice filling the room.

STRANGER

There is a stranger in this house, she says.
All night, something pacing the hall.
And this morning,
fresh water pooling in the drain,
a smudge left on a water glass.
Hand over those car keys —
If I only knew this would be the end,
you asking for the alphabet and *who is president,*
you haven't even checked the locks
or the closet, you don't understand
it feels like my head is underwater,
Hand me my shoes,
I am better, see,
this room, yes, this room:
the TV, the rocking chair,
the mirror over the couch.
I'll put the water on for coffee, forget
I even mentioned it. Last night
I had the most incredible dream.
Where did you find these? she says,
These shoes are not mine.

MY FATHER DIGGING UP
HIS GARDEN

Not enough,
this dusk crouching

in the season's slanting light.
The death sticks to you —

It's dark cling slinks beneath
your fingernail. Who will console you

when the squashes' flesh turns
the color of acid?

When the last
tomato drops off?

The wind moves in,
clipping off names

cell by cell —
How you are silenced

by these endings
the slow stirring of papery leaves.

No voice,
no pigment, no possibility,

no simple dying.

CHRISTMAS 2001, HANNAH
FALLS OFF THE ROOF

Not even the weight of a fallen body
could have cracked the ice that Christmas.
Ice that immured even the grass blades, and encased
the pine needles like thermometers.

Later, we joke about Hannah's
Santa Claus impression, only that wasn't it at all.
She only wanted to smoke a cigarette,

climbing through the kitchen window of her second floor
apartment, careful not to spill the red wine
on the linoleum, tear a hole in her stocking.

In the hospital room it didn't look like her,
eyes flooded shut like two bulbous halves of a plum,
thick white bandage wrapped in layers
around her head, blood seeping through like a threat.

I didn't speak. I wasn't there to stop her
from stepping onto the porch roof, to say,
this is another one of our bad ideas,
like the time we covered the kitchen floor

with dish soap and took running starts
from the dining room – two young girls
in feet pajamas betting on who could slide the furthest.

To this day, people look at the scar on my chin
with a look that says, *you were asking for it.*
I imagine the cold black shingles
were as slick and as uncertain as that soap.

I didn't even ask why she couldn't have just smoked inside,
instead I was the little sister who brought the mail
after the wounds were soothed,
wrist snapped back into place.

Even then, her eyes were still crooked,
one that looked forward, another that flickered up
to the ceiling not ready to come back.

No one looks at me the same, she said.
The ice didn't give me time to think.
It's like it was meant to happen. Ice,
the color of a belt buckle —
they look at me as if I jumped, she said.

ALZHEIMER'S FAITH

In my last hour,
I am only a throat

needing relief. I would swallow
any tablet with the promise

of memory. Is this God
catching in my blood,

while this last thought
clings to my underskin?

I pluck prayers
from my bones — what is left

flutters out of an empty drum.
I Hail Mary, Hail Mary,

Let my beads click off the last word.

PAPER BREATH

Dry and dusty
writer, how your lips forget

themselves, how your voice
has taken you by the tongue.

Words like tiny crosses
on the side of the road

crumble and crawl
into your mouth.

My God, you better cling
to those bones,

you better write your name down
on paper and swallow it.

THE ITCH

it doesn't scare me
the snake of this world
what's veinpopping hot
and unholy doesn't scare me
there is still something
new to this country
the whorey smell of big cities
a strange flower in some moth
eaten cow town
I don't want to go on
a rotten huddle of roots
a speck on this sad red earth
I bend my mind
to the rolling pavement
press my skin to the dash
and the streets will darken
with visions and loud voices
until they don't
and that's what fear is
not enough night
no more towns no west
just ocean

RED AFTERNOON

the pillow was thick
with interruptions first
the rusty shower pipes
across the ceiling
and then the stutter
of a pigeon outside
the window and I thought
this must be the middle
of America where you disappear
I was faceless to the noises
crawling in the wind
that worried loose through
the door smelling of corn and oil
I didn't see my initials
among the letters that burned
above the bed I had no eyes
anyway the sun moved in heavy
and strange like a sun meant
for some other person
and that's when I knew
I was alive when that red
light came barreling in as bold
as my vanishing my bones
no more a body
if not the shape of knees
beneath the sheets

AT THE DINER

you looked at me as if
you never thought I was capable
of such insults
and then stormed out hot
shouldered against the waitress
your full plate sitting there
steam breaking against the lamp
above the table
you go to cry about it
but you wouldn't have made that crack
about me getting old if you knew
that all I do is die
I don't even know myself
anymore because of it
you can't just walk out of here because
I stared at your back in the parking lot
and then I looked at your plate
full of meat and everything fell apart in me
I never told you about
the time in Denver 1949 it was spring
and the flowers were everywhere
I wanted a woman
I wanted it all and so I walked
at dusk looking for home
how I ached that night
at the lights edging the houses
and down at 23 and Welton
there was a softball game full
of happy families everywhere

and all I did was die
over and over until finally
I just walked away
to this day all I can think about
is the sadness of those floodlights
and you look at me my plate now empty
a beast with roast beef sitting
heavy in my stomach untouched
food now cold and taken away
but don't talk to me about getting old
you wouldn't if you understood that day
I looked behind me and all my bridges were gone

PRAYER

I spend the morning moving

the only way I know how — fingers pulling

at the edge of things — *there is dampness*

in the dishtowel, adjust the curtains, throw these papers

away. I am an error, a complaint

in the floorboards astonished by it's own refusing.

Just put your hands on something, I think,

and I move faster, I can't get myself clean enough.

I felt you coming — the pulp of your gap preceding you

like a cellar mouth, and now I cannot rid myself

of this single prayer, the smell of sour metal

on the porcelain — Dear God.

IT JUST HAPPENED

They dropped
into the yard —

hundreds of blackbirds landing
like handfuls of gravel.

There was nothing to make
of their constellations —

not a single perfect wing touching
a single perfect wing.

Then they scattered
unsure of what they took

with them.
I like this story.

Sometimes I can't say the words
fast enough.

MILL RUINS

I don't know why I didn't fuck you
on the deserted floor of that mill building,

the windows were indifferent,
an assembly line of unneeded light.

That's how it is with this city. The canals
fill and empty, sediment

clinging to ritual, walls defeated
by their own duration. I want to tell you

how it feels to be forgotten,
to disappear behind the slouch

of aging wood, but there is something
breaking in my mouth.

In a parking lot
with one hand under my dress, you say

let's just make love, let's blow
this whole damn thing out of the water,

but we don't —
but not for your marriage.

Standing among the mill ruins
there is a silence so fleshy, almost human,

the kind that waits
for something to happen.

Look at the way the city ignores even this.

AT THE BLUE MOON STRIP CLUB

I am watching a woman without breasts
step lightly around the stage,

piece by piece her skin announcing
itself. He says, the more you leave out,

the more she'll do, handing me
a stack of bills from his wallet.

He is an animal, an omen,
a vein beneath my tongue,

but I place two bills on the stage
anyway. She crawls toward me,

stopping only to run her hands
along her midsection, rubbing the two

triangular tan lines that frame her nipples.
You are cute, she says and removes

her panties. He watches me
as she lays down on her back,

legs spread in front of my face, slow
and cautious like clock hands.

LETTERS

It was easy
to lock them in the safe —

pale and luckless
as the bills, vanished

into the back of the closet.

Sometimes I still picture you running
down the streets of Lowell,

past the arena, the Brewery,
the Aiken Street Bridge.

Throw all my letters away.

49

NORTHERN CANAL

Standing by the Northern Canal
I have nothing to tell you.

Cars race by useless
water and debris clings

heavy on the surface.
I do not mention

the contract I still keep,
your agreement to attend AA,

your promise
to the doctor not to die.

I do not speak —
let the city

make its city sounds.
It was a joke to us then.

TO THE MAN WHO SAYS HE WILL
KILL HIMSELF AT 40

You tell your stories as if you know
they'll be forgotten. You find relief

in your mark that just won't take.
I remember that summer

you only took pictures of closed doors,
you gave all your books

away, you said all you need is a table
with one plate, with one humiliated chair.

No wife, no Wright,
no Kafka — what did it matter?

Ash flanks the doors of every building
you've ever walked though.

Once in a car in the rain, even your tongue
tasted of something burnt,

of something breaking. I do not know you,
I do not know you even now.

PRAYER

Tonight, I am noosing the marigolds

to force the life out.

It is almost winter. Outside,

a woman is thumbing through

my trash — breasts falling

out of a torn sweatshirt, bottles clanging

like altar bells. I can feel you in the road

beaten with wetness, and the trees not quite dead

with season — but to this woman,

I doubt your proof would be sufficient.

I have a story for you —

Once, I met a man who drew lines across his flesh

with a knife. He lifted his shirt to show me the scars,

perfect and precise, like scales on a fish.

And I could not stop picturing my body

on his body, his marked flesh pinned

by the suffocating cave of my mouth.

Dear God: I love your ugliness —

look how you arrive through these slender extrusions,

how you sour the air, barely even a breath

to you. Talk darkly to me.

DEAR LOWELL

I have decided to leave.
Bought a log home in the country —
a few extra rooms and a half-acre in the back.

I left you a man on a downtown sidewalk, a poem
tucked within a park bench. In the Highlands
neighborhood there is an empty apartment
and an endless breath of cars passing.

I could tell stories.

How I watched the sun crawl across the Merrimack —
buttoning and unbuttoning to let my body
flood with that disappointed light.
I walked down too many alleyways alone,
looked the wrong people in the eye and dared

the knife to my throat.
(Outside — frog sounds swell in unison.
And for hours, this will be all that happens.)

I could forget everything.

Trim back the roses, try and rake you out of my yard,
I could light a fire, toss in some love letters,
let the heat burn off the cheapness of my heart.

NOTES

In "June, on the Aiken Street Bridge" the line "your final hours written in water" is inspired by John Keats's tombstone epitaph: "Here lies one whose name was writ in water."

"June, on the Aiken Street Bridge" is for Tom Preble.

"Grandmother" and "Alzheimer" are for Eunice Sweeney.

In "Sybil Growing Smaller" the line "aloft in liquid air" is from Virgil's *Aeneid*.

"The Itch," "Red Afternoon," and "At the Diner" are all written after Jack Kerouac's *On the Road*.

ACKNOWLEDGMENTS

Grateful acknowledgment is made to the editors of the
following journals and anthologies where these poems,
sometimes in earlier versions, first appeared:

American Poetry Journal: "Mill City"

Bennington Review: "Prayer (3)," "Eve's Faith," "Paper Breath"

California Quarterly: "From the Bedroom"(Originally titled
"Mid Drift"), "My Mother's Faith"

Comstock Review: "Our Father"

Harpur Palate: "Major's"

Hobble Creek Review: "Riverwalk," "June on the Aiken Street
Bridge," "The Merrimack"

Knockout Magazine: "Prayer"

Where the Road Begins: "Confession"

Pebble Lake Review: "The Lost Tomb of Jesus"

Poet Lore: "Dear Lowell"

Wilderness House Review: "Woodworker," "Christmas 2001,
Hannah Falls Off the Roof"

Thank you to my family and to the following friends and writers who provided their support and comments regarding the poems in this collection, without whom this book would not be possible: Michael Burkard, Amy Gerstler, Major Jackson, Timothy Liu, Paul Marion from Loom Press, Michael Paglia, and Dave Robinson.

My thanks to the Bennington Writing Seminars community and the encouragement of my dear friends: Stacy Magner Barrett, Mary Saunders Dawson, and A.N. Devers.

Specific thanks to Denny Ludvino for our long friendship and for generously designing this book.

Finally, to Bert Foster for your endless support through all these years — In the words of another poet:

> *When I mention the word love,*
> *keeping it on my tongue,*
> *you say, Yes —*

KATE HANSON FOSTER gained her MFA in Poetry from the Bennington Writing Seminars. Her poetry has appeared in *California Quarterly, Comstock Review, Harpur Palate, Poet Lore* and elsewhere. She lives and writes in Groton, Massachusetts.

This book is set in Mrs Eaves, a typeface designed by Zuzana Licko in 1996. Mrs Eaves is based on type cut by the 18th-century English printer and punchcutter John Baskerville. It is named after Sarah Eaves, Baskerville's housekeeper, aide, and mistress.